By Johann H. Diemer

D1741803

NATURE
&
MIRACLE

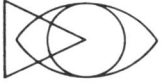

Wedge Publishing Foundation, Toronto, Canada
1977

Copyright © 1977 Wedge Publishing Foundation, 229 College
St., Toronto, Ontario, Canada M5T 1R4. All rights reserved.

ISBN 0-88906-015-0

This book is a translation by Wilma Bouma of Part I of **Natuur en
Wonder,** published in Amsterdam in 1963 by Buijten en Schipperheijn
in the series **Christelijk Perspectief** edited by Johan Stellingwerff.
Part II of that volume gives a systematic and historical treatment
of the subject. Part I was originally published in 1944 in **Orgaan
van de Christelijke Vereniging van Natuur- en Geneeskundigen.**
Dooyeweerd's memorial piece first appeared in 1949 in
Philosophia Reformata.

Design: Anthony Goodhoofd Associates
Printed in Canada

Contents

Foreword

This essay by the late Harry Diemer, though conceived well over thirty years ago, deserved to be made available in the English language if only because it treats topics that continue to occupy the minds of believers in a way that is not generally accessible to the English reading public. Besides being novel, Diemer's treatment is, more importantly, helpful as well. The topics that I have in mind have always aroused great interest, have engendered heated debates, and are often taken as shibboleths of christian orthodoxy in one quarter or another. They are: the reality and nature of miracles, the relation of faith to healing, creation and evolution, creation and redemption, and similar ones.

There are, of course, characteristics of this essay that date it, but it is not for that reason outdated. There are also characteristics that are typically continental, but it is not for that reason useless to the Anglo-Saxon mind. Its datedness appears here and there in the acceptance of problem formulations or problem solutions that many today would experience as scholastic. Its continental orientation is especially evident in the lack of argumentation. But for a reader prepared to search beyond these minor irritations for a contemporary mind, there awaits the discovery of a christian thinker of stature, whose ideas have a scope and depth that can but enrich the inquisitive reader and that will allow us to look at certain traditional problems with a degree of freshness that is sure to advance discussion.

So far from being traditional is this essay that at first it does not at all strike one as dealing with these '' worn out'' topics mentioned above, but rather seems a theologico-philosophical essay on the essential characteristics of nature. The author sets forth a basic cosmology, attempts to ground that in the christian faith, and then tries to find out how our concept of the miraculous fits in. His analysis is heavily indebted to the style of christian thinking that is today closely associated with Amsterdam and Toronto. Technical tools developed in that tradition, such as the concepts of the law-subject relation and the subject-object relation, obviously have served Diemer well in his study, even though he does not work with them in a jargonistic way that would make his suggestions enigmatic to the uninitiated reader.

In the treatment of others who have also dealt with his interests, the reader will find Diemer fair and ecumenical. He shares with us his appreciation for their contributions and also points out how his own views may do more justice to difficulties not overcome so far. He displays that originality of mind that does not depend on the excommunication of other minds. And in all this, one is continually struck by how scholarly brilliance in philosophical, theological, and biological matters is naturally and pastorally interwoven with a concern for the practical problems of the christian faith.

To me the book seems strongest at its weakest point. That weakness is encountered in the notion that the primary meaning of what is miraculous is to be found in the idea that all of God's works are wondrous. For the weakness of this is that if all things have a certain character, no thing in particular will stand out in having that character. And one then wonders whether floating axes, walking on water, sticks becoming snakes, and dead people being called back to life are in any way peculiar or outstanding or different? And if so, are they like all other events in being miraculous? God, according to Diemer's interpretation of the world in the light of Scripture, is always actively present in all that occurs in the world. It is not true that he sometimes intervenes and at other times not. What is miraculous to us is due to the fact that the Word, which sets the pattern of God's continuous and active presence, is not only beyond our understanding, but also transcends all that it at the same time makes possible.

I am not persuaded that Diemer himself gets out of this problem in a clearly presented solution. But I do think that the makings of the solution are present in his suggestions. They are present in the notion that God as the author of creation, as the one who calls it forth and sustains it in his call, is not like creatures subject to his commands. His commands originate in him. Would he in dealing with creatures not be able to do far more with them than they themselves could do or even fathom? And would he not for the sake of their salvation want to make that point especially clear at times? Most of what we notice of his activity is so familiar to us that we think we fathom it. Sometimes what he does breaks through that familiarity. Sometimes he makes sure that he comes through in that way.

The notion of the miraculous is a notion that is closely related to the notion of explanation. Some things are easy to explain. Some things are hard to explain. Some things we cannot explain at all. And the only word of explanation we can offer in the face of some claims, to go yet one step further, is that they must be false because what is said to have happened cannot have happened. And when we nevertheless accept that it happened, we say that we accept a miracle. We can easily explain why it is that most plants will die without regular intake of water. We find it difficult to explain the formula $E = mc^2$. We are unable to explain why people who smoke much get cancer more easily than others. And if some person claims that he saw a steel axehead floating in his bathtub, we explain that it cannot be. Yet when a prophet claims that he saw an axehead float in water, we accept it and say it was a miracle.

Diemer's essay helps us come to grips with this problem. He does so by introducing certain concepts of creation, by relating the problem to our faith, by reintroducing the demonic into our experience, and so forth. He also does it by asking us to drop certain notions, in particular the one of the supernatural. All of this is of great importance for the christian academic, because academic life lives off explaining. It is also important for the christian believer, because he wants to accept miracles as integral to his faith. Diemer helps both by suggesting that no individual creaturely event can be reduced to its explanation ever. He also helps by pointing out that though explanation is related to seeing patters of order, the origin of these patterns is always beyond explanation. If miraculous means "beyond explanation", God's order is a miracle and so is every individual event in its individuality. What we can "explain" is those events that we have learned to relate to the order that has become familiar to us.

Diemer's thinking has proven to be stimulating and clarifying to me without leaving me with the dreary spectre of a solution to all problems. May the reader find that these pages advance discussion and support the faith.

Hendrik Hart
Fall 1977.

In memory of Johann "Harry" Heinrich Diemer

When we of the editorial board of *Philosophia Reformata* received official word on October 4, 1948 that "Harry" Diemer had passed away in June of 1945, we lost a thinker whose name will always be bound up with our journal and also with the Association for Calvinistic Philosophy. Our editorial board thus lost its very capable secretary, who had served in this capacity since the journal's inception in 1936. I lost a friend of very exceptional stature, who was at the same time one of my best co-workers and whose early life held great promise for the future.

Johann Heinrich Diemer was born on November 7, 1904 in Dronrijp, a town in the northern Dutch province of Friesland. His father was the Rev. N. Diemer, who last served the Reformed [Gereformeerd] church at Vijfhuizen and who was himself an important member of the Association for Calvinistic Philosophy for a considerable period of time.

Harry — as his friends called him — attended the christian lyceum at Haarlem and completed his final examinations there in 1925. He then went on to study biology at the University of Leiden. Because of the spiritual intensity of his character, his elevated, christian view of life, and his continual struggle with the problem of the relation between science and the christian religion, he soon became prominent in the student life of the Reformed Student Movement. He had very diligently studied the ideas of Abraham Kuyper, Herman Bavinck, and Jan Woltjer on the question of science and religion; even after he became an adherent of the philosophy of the cosmonomic idea, he still had considerable difficulty in letting go of the doctrine of the *logos*, which played such a large role in the thought of Woltjer in particular. As Diemer more than once explained, this doctrine had worked its way very deeply into his spirit. But the neo-scholastic line in calvinistic thinking left him unsatisfied from the very beginning. With penetrating insight he saw the hidden dualism in this way of thinking, and the young, radical thinker felt driven in his heart to seek a reformational conception of reality in which this dualism would be overcome.

Diemer thus became a seeker who opened himself up on all sides to new intellectual streams from all directions. His sharp, penetrating intellect was weighed down by a turbulent inner life; the unsolved problems kept him in a state of continual emotional tension and caused a deep unrest in his life. It was in these circumstances that he became acquainted with the new calvinistic philosophy through a course I was teaching in Leiden at that time. My *Wijsbegeerte der Wetsidee* [the Dutch first edition of *A New Critique of Theoretical Thought*] had not yet appeared, but he studied with concentrated attention everything that had been published up to that time and immediately sought personal contact with me.

Under the supervision of Professor Boschma, Diemer was working on a dissertation entitled *Over biotypen van Anopheles maculipennis Meigen, in het bijzonder in Westelijk Nederland. Een taxonomisch onderzoek* [*On Biotypes of Anopheles maculipennis Meigen, Particularly in the Western Netherlands: A Taxonomic Investigation*]. This subject forced him to undertake extensive experimental research and involved him in his favourite field of study, theoretical biology in which his interest had been aroused especially by Van der Klaauw, one of his professors at Leiden. In the eighth chapter of the dissertation entitled "Over het karakter van de realiteit van biotypen en typenkringen" ["On the Character of the Reality of Biotypes and Type-Spheres], he had an opportunity to work with me theory of individuality structures and their interlacements, within the framework of a philosophical exposition of the concepts of species, class, and type in biology. This was a first attempt to make this theory fruitful for theoretical investigation in biological science, and I had encouraged him very much in this direction. He also received stimulating, encouraging interest from Professor van der Klaauw, who had immediately gauged Diemer's philosophical aptitude.

On July 5, 1935 Diemer received his doctorate with honours under Professor Boschma. Then a difficult period for this young scholar began, a period in which his character was to undergo the most severe tests. He had found an ideal for his life and wanted to strive toward it, unselfishly abandoning his own interests. A reformational christian vision of reality had been opened to him, and he hoped to work it out in the area of biological science and to use his philosophical vision as the foundation for a programme of empirical biological research. He had become completely convinced of the truth that every theory in the special sciences rests on philosophical — and, in the deepest sense, religious — presuppositions. But because of this insight, he came into sharp conflict with the dominant spirit among biological scientists, both of humanistic and of christian persuasion. This young, enthusiastic thinker simply was not understood. From various sides people hinted that if he did not want to spoil completely his career as a biologist, he should abandon his philosophical aspirations and should limit himself to the problems of biological science. They seemed to think that Diemer had chosen some sort of aprioristic philosophical biology for his life-work and had rejected research in his area.

His teacher Van der Klaauw was the only one in the circle of biologists who seemed to understand Diemer fully. He would gladly have offered him some sort of scientific position at the University of Leiden, but he lacked the means to do so. Diemer did assist his teacher in an unofficial way with the *Acta Biotheoretica*, but this naturally brought him little financial gain. Professor van der Klaauw was continually on the lookout for a scientific position for this promising young scholar, a position to which his abilities entitled him. Finally he wrote me that the Free University of Amsterdam should lay claim to this accomplished scientist, for it would not easily find another biologist of such abilities.

However, the Free University's young faculty of mathematics and natural sciences appeared to have no place in its originally modest circle for a biologist. Other attempts to find a place for Diemer were no more successful. Moreover, it quickly became apparent that Diemer's philosophical convictions were not regarded as a point in his favour. It was one of the bitterest experiences of my life to see how my young co-worker, with whom I had already entered into a warm friendship, everywhere met with the same misunderstandings that I knew so well from my own experience. But it was just in this period which was so disappointing for Diemer that the strength of his christian faith and the unselfishness of his character revealed themselves most fully.

When his original hope of being able to devote himself completely to scientific study vanished he accepted it immediately as God's guidance in his life. He then threw himself with full dedication and energy into a teaching position, which would at least provide him with a temporary way to make a living.

In his free time Diemer lovingly devoted his attention to the Association for Calvinistic Philosophy, which had been established in 1935, and to its journal *Philosophia Reformata*. He became secretary of the editorial board of the journal and also served on the executive board of the association. In the first year of publication of *Philosophia Reformata*, an article by Diemer appeared under the title "Het soortbegrip en de idee van het constante structuurtype in de biologie" ["The Concept of Species and the Idea of a Constant Structure-Type in Biology"]. From a calvinistic philosophical standpoint, this article must still be regarded as breaking new ground in the field. It was followed by a series of other articles in which he developed his ideas in even fuller and more mature form. I would point in particular to his detailed study on "De totaliteitsidee in de biologie en de psychologie" ["The Idea of Totality in Biology and Psychology"] in *Philosophia Reformata* in 1939. In this article he also included the area of animal psychology in his investigation, which he had earlier touched on in a short study entitled "Arbeidsveld, taak en methode der dierenpsychologie" ["Field of Investigation, Task, and Method of Animal Psychology"], published in *Philosophia Reformata* in 1937. He had also dealt with animal psychology in a lecture entitled "De nieuwe holistische biologie" ["The New Holistic Biology"], which he delivered to the Christian Association for Natural and Medical Sciences and published in 1936 in the journal of that association. This lecture is of particular importance because it examines extensively the newer attempts to develop an intrinsic biologicalonathematics, attempts that I had only been able to make allusions to in the second volume of my *Wijsbegeerte der Wetsidee*. Also worthy of particular mention is Diemer's detailed treatment of "Wijsgeerige biologie van Thomistisch en Calvinistisch Standpoint" ["Philosophical Biology from a Thomistic and a Calvinistic Standpoint"], which was published in the journal of the Christian Association for Natural and Medical Sciences in 1938.

In various excellent reviews in *Philosophia Reformata* of newly published works in the areas of theoretical and philosophical biology, Diemer demonstrated that he continued to follow and master the literature with intensive interest. Many will still remember his splendid lectures on the state of the problem of evolution and his rejection of the scholastic accommodation standpoint on the basis of a reformational view of the Scriptures. Because of Diemer's penetrating critical analysis of the existing evidence, his lectures on evolution brought us much further in our understanding of the problem. How well he was able to dominate his audience with his fiery spirit and the inspiration of his scriptural vision of science!

Meanwhile, Diemer's financial difficulties were growing. He was married and had formed a family. His temporary teaching position came to an end, and all his attempts to secure a teaching position in some other educational institution were unsuccessful. In this critical situation Professor van der Klaauw again proved himself to be a true friend. Through van der Klaauw's efforts, Diemer was able to get a position as an assistant in the laboratory for anatomy and embryology at the University of Groningen. But here difficulties of an entirely different nature awaited him. Professor de Burlet, the man under whom Diemer worked in this laboratory, was an adherent of National Socialist principles, and he attempted to influence Diemer in this direction. De Burlet's friendly manner toward his assistant at a time when virtually everyone else seemed to have deserted him aroused in the sensitive and impulsive Diemer a strong attachment to this scholar, who reciprocated. At the same time, there were growing conflicts between the two as Diemer sharply resisted the National Socialist influence.

When he remained in de Burlet's laboratory during the German occupation of the Netherlands in the second world war, completely ungrounded suspicions began to arise. On one occasion in 1943 when Diemer came to visit me, I discussed this matter with him. He was immediately convinced that under the circumstances he must break with Professor de Burlet, however much this might conflict with his strong personal attachment to the man. On the very same day — typical of his character — he wrote to de Burlet to tell him that he would not return to Groningen. I had already guessed his plans. From now on Harry Diemer would throw himself with all his unselfish energy into the resistance movement. When my suspicions were confirmed, a secret fear came over me that now we would quickly lose him for good. Because I knew his character, I realized that he would not hide from danger.

On January 24, 1945 Diemer was arrested, and on March 17 he was sent to the notorious concentration camp at Neuengamme. From there he went to Hamburg and finally to Sandborstel, where he died in the month of June at the age of 40 in a British hospital, after having been liberated by the English on April 29.

Diemer's father wrote me the following description of the last days of his life: "I can share with you that during his days as a prisoner he showed the same dedication to his fellow prisoners that he had always shown to others in all his work. He comforted the dying, helped the sick, and even shared his own scanty rations with them. Every day he gave lectures on philosophical subjects in order to keep his fellow prisoners busy and to direct their attention away from their plight. For many prisoners this was a rich blessing, as some who have survived have told us."

In *Philosophia Reformata* in 1943-44 Diemer had given us perhaps his deepest and most mature work on the subject of nature and wonder. In an extensive series of studies he posed and treated this problem in an entirely new way. Unfortunately, the conclusion of this series could not be published, because the Gestapo seized the last copy during its raid of Diemer's home in Groningen.

Thus this young life was cut off. Many of his colleagues in biology had seen in him only an "idealist" who had spoiled his own future through his philosophical aspirations. But those who have truly known what it was that inspired the life of this youthful and talented fighter realize that it was from no "idealism" up in the clouds that he received the strength to give himself entirely to his calling while completely ignoring his own interests. Anyone who studies the writings that Diemer left behind must conclude that he made an earnest attempt at reformed science in the area of biology — an attempt that puts many Christians to shame.

And so Harry Diemer's person and work will live on among us as a stimulating example for all who in true self-denial and in the power of christian faith are prepared to walk the thorny path of *scientia reformata*, a path whose beginning holds nothing but disappointment, misunderstanding, and opposition. But the steadfast pursuit of this course brings with it the prospect of great blessing, for *la vérité est en marche et rien ne l'arrêtera*. And those who fought in the front lines of this battle will not be forgotten by later generations that will pluck the fruits of their work.

God's design

Following Calvin, we have a concept of nature which embraces *all* of creation. For Calvin, nature is an order established by God within which all his works are enacted. We cannot separate the development of God's works in time from the divine world order. All things lie enclosed in this order as an integrated whole before they are unfolded by God in time after the six-day creation act.

From the beginning the Word is with God, is God, and precedes the creation act; in the Word God has his design and purpose for the world, his creation, before him from eternity. In that design God prescribed the world's entire development in time down to the last detail. This prescription, however, is not of a causal nature but affects things in their coherence and inter-relationships. What man differentiates as cause and effect, as before and after, God knows simultaneously and surveys as a whole. The prescription is from eternity, from beforehand; the ordered whole, the decree of God, comes before the execution. It is created "in the beginning" — that is, in the Word, the root or radical base of everything in creation — as "heaven and earth."

This "beforehand" is a distinction made by human thought bound to time which can understand the works of God only with the concepts of "before and after", "earlier and later", "first and following". The decree, the creation, and the unfolding in time are one and the same for God in his Word. Only in man's thinking does the decree precede the six-day creation of the world order, and the creation act the unfolding of creation in time. What is really a coherent whole appears to human consciousness separated into a series of acts. This is the way man acquires insight into the structure and direction of creation.

There is a fundamental difference between God's design and a man's design. A man needs a certain amount of time both to draw up a design and to execute it. Whether it be to build a house, manufacture a product, or write a book, a plan is always made up of a series of decisions in a certain sequence in which any decision always joins onto and presupposes what went before. The means needed to carry out the plan are chosen and designed for that purpose. The ultimate goal of the design is always primary. Thus a builder always directs the forces at work and uses the tools so

1

that the final results correspond to what the architect intended in the first place.

It is entirely different with God's design. Here we cannot speak of a series of decisions — of an initial decision followed by subordinate decisions — which all serve to reach the ultimate goal. God's decision is of one piece. One single decision embraces the entire cosmos with its abiding law structures, enclosed in the religious root of nature, and the creatures and events subject to these abiding norms.[1] God has been carrying out his design from the beginning; he is engaged in establishing his decree. The execution of the design consists of the six-day creation of the temporal order and the unfolding in cosmic time of everything that is subjectively enclosed in it. Both the act of creation and the unfolding always point to the Creator. Indeed God does not set himself objectives which he can reach only via specific means. His purpose is in himself, in his own glory and perfection. To the creation, however, God has given a task, which must be carried out in the course of time with power which he supplies.

God's activity is never subjected to duration of time, neither "in the beginning" and in the six-day creation act nor in the unfolding and the re-creation. Time began with the rest on the seventh day. In the established world order the unfolding of creation and the redemption from sin takes place in time. In God's consciousness creation and re-creation are one. It is only in man's consciousness, bound as it is to time, that creation comes first and contains within it the possibility of a fall and a re-creation.

Creation

God's creative work "in the beginning" is an all-inclusive design. Out of the fulness of his power and wisdom, God designs and creates the realms of heavenly spirits, men, animals, plants, and elements — all in mutual coherence as one vast kingdom. First God creates each realm according to its basic structure, which is subsequently worked out in types and subtypes. Together these creatures form a definite structural relationship in time. Within this structure innumerable creatures function in the course of time. This all-embracing totality of creation, this heaven and earth, is rooted in God's Word, in Christ, before the beginning of the six-day creation act.

According to Scripture, the creation of all this, of "heaven and earth," took place "in the beginning." We are dealing here with an expression of time that functions in our faith. Created man, who looks for the origin of all things, is shown the creative work of God as the beginning of all things and as the act whereby the whole of creation was called into being. This act took place "in the beginning," that is, in God's Word, in Christ who can only be acknowledged *in faith*. Jesus Christ stands not only at the end but also at the beginning of all things. He is the absolute fulfillment of all time and also the absolute beginning.

The divine process of creation is history. This must be understood as primordial history. The Creator did not require a period of time in order to create the world. Rather, time became through the act of creation. Human consciousness functions in time and therefore can understand the creative work of God only if it is laid out in a number of acts to each of which is ascribed a certain portion of created time along with the enclosed creation ordinances and the concrete creatures belonging to it. Consequently, in the creation account the announcement of the order in which God has created all things is suited to the needs of human understanding. In the days is enclosed all that becomes after the creation — all that shall appear during the unfolding process in the course of cosmic time. Not one of these days can be dissociated from the beginning in which they are all initially enclosed and from which they appear before man's eye.

The days are also moments of beginning. As such they are absolute; that is, we cannot think of any created time prior to them. Each day is the beginning of a particular creation norm and reveals another facet of the whole creation, which then becomes richer and more complete until in man its fulness is revealed completely before our eyes. The days cannot be thought of as separated from each other. They cannot be seen as coming one after the other in a continuous stream of cosmic time in a predetermined sequence in which they could be fenced off from each other. The view that the days coincide with certain periods of time has the consequence that they must have been a certain length, be it long or short, and that they lie behind us in the more or less distant past.

This conception, however, does great injustice to the nature of the days. They do not coincide with certain long or short periods of cosmic time. As Augustine already realized, they have an altogether different meaning. They are basically dateless and cannot be measured by any human standard of time measurement.

In our interpretation of the days, however, their reality-character [*realiteitskarakter*] is maintained; this is not the case in the conception of the days as periods of time. What then is the reality-character of the days? Just as "in the beginning" presents to our view the *totality* of creation, so the six days show us the *temporal arrangements* of the created world, which cannot be conceived of apart from the totality. The days have not gone by any more than has the beginning; on the contrary, they are still present and real. Just as the beginning of creation is continually present in the all-embracing whole, so also the days are present in the *fundamental structures* of the various realms. These structures cannot be thought of as separate from the concrete creatures and their relationships in the passage of time.

It is within these structures that the biologist and geologist first distinguish certain temporal periods which mark the opening up of concrete creation in cosmic time. Thus the geologist divides the history of the earth into three eras: the Paleozoic, the Mesozoic, and the Cenozoic. Each of these eras is divided again into a number of periods such as the Cambrian, the Silurian, the Devonian, and so on. Furthermore, the biologist recognizes in the history of the numerous branches of living things an initial phase, a developmental phase, and an end phase. All these time periods and phases can be expressed in terms of time measurement.

However, the days cannot be measured by any standard. Each day is the beginning of the basic structure of a new realm of creatures; it is a new structure of the temporal order, giving a new completeness to temporal duration. Within each day, from the very moment of its origin, the creatures can function as within an abiding creation order. For as soon as the arrangement is placed in time, the unfolding in cosmic time can begin. Thus in the six days the creation order, without which a world history is impossible, is placed in time. In the account of creation this future history is anticipated. Again and again after the creating Word has first been spoken, it is said that the earth and the sea brought forth living things which multiplied each according to its kind. The appearance and development of the creatures in the passage of time can be separated neither from the created structure nor from the entire creation. As the days are always present in the order, so the beginning is always present in the totality and fulness of God's plan.

The creation unfolds

The execution in time of the creation design is the unfolding of the actual creatures and their relationships within the creation order.

Every beginning of a new phylum of plants or animals on earth is an *absolute* beginning, for it is based on creation. Therefore, by "beginning" we do not understand a certain abstract moment of time in the history of the world which can be dated but rather the created typical fundamental structure, a temporal structure, with which the phylum appears on earth. The evolutionism of Haeckel and others has completely denied the existence of these typical structures and thereby made living processes autonomous. It absolutized them into a so-called natural creative process, a concept used in naturalism and pantheism. But without these created structural complexes no development or disclosure of the individual forms of life is possible. Whatever appears in the course of time always appears within certain structures; potentially it already lies enclosed within these structures and cannot go beyond the boundaries they set.

To say that the beginning of a new phylum is grounded in creation means in no way that God created in a supernatural way by intervening in independent natural events. Anyone who thinks it does begins with an autonomous natural process wherein he then allows God to introduce something new from the outside. This way of thinking is not in line with Scripture. We have to start with the creative work of God in the beginning and during the six days.

All that appears new in cosmic time is being driven out of the religious root of nature wherein it is enclosed by creation. Nothing which appears can be separated from the whole, from the planned unity of all things which extends from the beginning to the end of time. Therefore, the appearance of something new is not the result of a power above and beyond nature bringing into it what was not there before. Rather, what is already there is disclosed through the subjective activity of individual creatures within created constant structures. This subjective activity is always correlated with certain possibilities that lie, objectively determined, in the creatures that already exist. The disclosure of these possibilities waits for the activity of higher subjects in the cosmos.

Anyone who has studied the history of life on earth and has noted the results of decades of paleontological research has time and again been confronted with the fact of the spontaneous appearance of plants and animals of a new type. In the appearance of these new types, one may clearly note a discontinuity and periodicity. Major groups appear suddenly and often disappear just as suddenly. The chief objection to the idea of gradual evolution among all of its critics is the lack of transitional forms between the big systematic groups (phyla, classes, orders, and sometimes even families).

During the Cambrian and Silurian periods, for example, the molluscs appear in six different types. From the outset they appear together; common progenitor specimens are not found. In the Silurian Period, sea urchins appear spontaneously in a number of species, genera, and families. The appearance of Ostracoderms in the Silurian Period is a most remarkable event in the history of the earth. They arise directly from an unknown origin in a broad spectrum of species and genera, provided with all sorts of protective equipment. Once the type has appeared, we see the drama of its development in time. Some sub-types initially develop further while others gradually disappear. Thus the

5

number of species and genera decreases gradually until at the end of the Devonian Period the entire group disappears.

Teleosts appear in the Devonian Period in many types. Similarly, reptiles emerge in the Triassic and Permian Periods. Leafy plants arise in the mid-Cretaceous Period, directly as monocotyledons and dicotyledons, and in a great variety of forms. Their genera have changed little down to the present time. In the beginning of the Tertiary Period nearly all the mammals appear, including carnivorous animals, bats, ungulates, elephants, water-buffaloes, rodents, seals, and primates (simians and pro-simians). The latter come on the scene in twenty-five genera and sixty species. We look in vain for transitional forms.

Furthermore, we can observe spontaneity in greater or lesser degree in the development within certain typical groups. In the history of many phyla we presently distinguish three phases. In the first phase the new fundamental type appears very suddenly and splits directly into many subtypes which are adapted to various environments. The diverse possibilities of the basic type are worked out while the fundamental framework is retained. Thus, for example, molluscs appear in six different kinds including gastropods, cephalopods, and lamellibranchs, which are impossible to reduce to a common source. If we follow the ancestral series back in time, they do converge more and more. But this convergence never crosses certain boundaries. We never find a real point of intersection for the different types which would be the basis for the sought-after ancestral form.

Whereas classes, orders, and families appear in the first phase, in the second phase these types are worked out in a number of genera and species in which the original line of development is continued to the end. This phenomenon is called orthogenesis. Within this second phase belong the well-known ancestral series such as those of horses and elephants. This is really the blooming phase of the series in which growth and maturation occur.

In the third phase the end of the series is reached, often beginning with a dissolution process. A certain restlessness and uncertainty is noticeable in the forms of this phase. We could say that speciation has "run wild." Individual forms become so variable that it becomes difficult to establish the typical boundaries of species. Along with this appear all sorts of pathological symptoms such as giant forms and the abnormal growth of certain parts of the body. It seems as if the individuals want to withdraw from the dominion of the law for their type. Examples of groups which disappeared entirely from the scene are four big groups of molluscs and five large groups of reptiles that all died out at the end of the Cretaceous Period.

The miracle of creation

The miracle of creation reveals itself in the spontaneity with which new types of creatures appear. We can speak of a miracle here because something new arises time and again; new structures appear which cannot be reduced to what came earlier. Scripture is our guide here. It speaks of the miraculous works of God, the great things which human thought cannot fathom. The starry sky, the earth, and the sea with their moving creatures all witness to the wondrous works of God. According to the Bible miracles are God's incomprehensible works not only of providence and re-creation but also of creation.

Almost a century ago, Hugh Miller, an amateur geologist, wrote from a christian perspective *The Footprints of the Creator*. In this stimulating and still worthwhile book, the author relates a conversation he had with a clergyman friend as they were walking over an ancient stony terrain that was full of fossils. The talk concerned the miracle of Pentecost. Miller remarked:

But what say you to the relics which stand out in such bold relief from the rocks beside us, in *their* character as the results of miracle? The perished tribes and races which they represent all *began* to exist. There is no truth which science can more conclusively demonstrate than that they all had a beginning. The infidel who, in this late age of the world, would attempt falling back on the fiction of an ''infinite series,'' would be laughed to scorn. They all began to be. But how? No true geologist holds by the development hypothesis — it has been resigned to sciolists and smatterers — and there is but one other alternative. They began to be, *through the miracle of creation.* From the evidence furnished by these rocks we are shut down either to the belief in *miracle*, or to the belief in something else infinitely harder of reception, and as thoroughly unsupported by testimony as it is contrary to experience. Hume is at last answered by the severe truths of the stony science. He was not, according to Job, ''in league with the stones of the field,'' and they have risen in irresistible warfare against him in the Creator's behalf.[2]

Miller wrote this before 1850. A century of geological and paleontological research has since then only confirmed his insight.

Acknowledging the miracle of creation, however, does not entail the notion that the Creator intervened in a supernatural way in the course of natural processes every time a new class of plants or animals appeared. In his book, Miller defends the concept that every new dynasty is called into existence by a direct intervention of God. Again and again, after ages during which no improvement occurred but rather degradation, the Word of creation was heard calling forth the appearance of a higher order of creatures. In this manner fish, creeping things, mammals, and finally man came into existence on earth. Miller thinks of the days of Genesis 1 as periods of time. He says that the Lord made heaven and earth in six time periods. Now God does not create new things anymore because his moral world-rule began with the seventh day. However, according to Miller, the creative work which led to a higher order of things and which kept the Creator busy for millions of years was of an ordinary work-a-day nature.

Miller confuses the creation with the unfolding in the process of time, which, as I have already pointed out earlier, can be divided into long periods. The six-day creation act, whereby the basic structures were created, is fundamental to the unfolding process. It makes this process possible but is not synonymous with it. He who thinks creation has taken place in the course of cosmic time and who at the same time also wants to do justice to the facts of geology and paleontology, as Miller does, has to conceive of the days as long periods of time. But, in so doing, he does injustice to the account of creation in which God, who in his creative work is not bound to time, simply communicates with man in a form suitable to the needs of human understanding.

Many paleontologists no longer think Darwinism and Lamarckism are hypotheses that can explain all. Instead they talk about "natural creative history" or about "natural creative development," which they see as a realization of new forms of life from *actual potencies*. This is analogous to the development (or ontology) of an individual organism. In the primordial organism, then, the potencies of all the types — that is, all phyla, classes, orders, families — would be enclosed.

In more recent times it is particularly H. Conrad-Martius who recognized that the history of life on earth cannot be understood without the acceptance of divine creation.[3] But Conrad-Martius considers this "potencies" interpretation absurd: such a primordial organism, which would have the entire living world potentially enclosed within it, would indeed be the "miracle of all miracles." According to her, we cannot avoid accepting a creation both of the form and matter of the fundamental types mentioned above. This "transcendental new creation" [*Erschaffung*], which occurs on the principle of direct intervention in natural happenings (supernatural divine deeds), has to be distinguished from immanent natural creative development by which all creatures (enclosed within the already mentioned types which had the potencies for all the families, species, and races) appeared during innumerable centuries. Races, species, and families can be part of a natural creation process whereby a phylum comes into being. In contrast, families, orders, classes, and phyla exist through creative form-giving and can never be part of a natural phyletic relationship.

Conrad-Martius does not, however, wish to say that only the fundamental types are included in the creation plan. The

8 Nature and Miracle

sub-types, in fact every individual creature, are also the result of the Creator's thought. In the eternal Word, the Logos, all types are enclosed as creation thoughts and they come to be in accordance with the essential order to which they belong, the former by a direct forming of the organism and the latter by natural empirical causes (mutations and so on).[4]

There are certainly worthwhile elements in these ideas of Conrad-Martius. She recognizes that not only the fundamental types but also the lower orders rest in creation. Furthermore, she sees that they are always realized in the concrete organism and its relationships. Like Miller, she considers every natural process separated from the foundation of creation a figment of the imagination.

On the other hand, the scholastic supernaturalism of Conrad-Martius must be refuted. She accepts the dualism of a divine creation plan and a relatively autonomous state of natural processes. In the former, the history of the world is thought out in advance and is fixed. In the latter, the Creator from time to time moves new orders (with the enclosed new possibilities for development) from the creation plan into the course of time. These then work themselves out independently through "natural creation processes." They are then, as the author says, "brought into operation."

Undoubtedly it is true that, while looking back upon the history of life in the world, we see new fundamental types emerge from time to time. These appear to be immediately worked out in various sub-types which are further particularized down to the elementary types of reproductive communities of racial groups. This phenomenon has already been demonstrated with examples. It is incorrect, however, to say that the Creator acted in an interfering, supernatural manner and allowed newly created things to appear at certain points in time. The new structural principles are not immaterial, metaphysical forms which come from outside of nature to direct material events. Rather, they are principles of structures which were worked out in the divine creation act and enclosed in the religious root of nature. The morphogenesis and development of the individual organism and its relationships cannot be separated from these structural principles. The result of both the initial and the six-day creation act lies as an absolute world order at the foundation of natural opening-up processes. Whenever the opening-up process begins to take place before our eyes, the creative work is completed.

Therefore, we may never think of the creative work of God as intervening in the course of cosmic time. Rather we must think of this work as having been done in the beginning and in the six days which precede the opening-up process and form its structural foundation in the religious root of nature. This foundation belongs to the totality of temporal reality.

Conrad-Martius separates these orderings from that root. She sees them as more or less independent "forms" which are brought into reality through divine creative acts. But God never works outside the root of nature. He created the orders by his Word and enclosed them in the Word as the root from which his Spirit brings forth the multiplicity of individual creatures in the course of time.

The miracle of creation lies in the spontaneous appearance of the structural principles within which the generations of creatures pass and through which the existence of these creatures becomes possible. Every structure founded in creation is a new beginning and is always present as the constant order in the changing genetic relationships so long as the species continues to exist on earth. Consequently, the miracle of its creation is continually present also.

This miracle is the miracle of existence which reveals itself in the innumerable forms and shapes of actual creatures and their relationships to each other in the course of time. These are *signs* in which the creation miracle becomes manifest to us, through which we first become aware of the miracle. Therefore, in all of nature nothing is excluded from this miracle; the one miracle of the created world order reveals itself in all things.

However, it is not only in non-living and living nature that the miracle of creation is revealed. We find it also in the history of man, in the works of government, culture, and technology. Here also new principles, the origins of which we cannot comprehend, occur again and again spontaneously and unexpectedly. They rise up out of dark depths and cannot be prevented from working their way to the fore. Think of the revolutions which herald new periods of history and introduce different ways of thought; of technical inventions which bring about social and economic revolutions; of scientific ideas which lead thought and research into new channels. After these appear they are worked out in the course of time. They are built up and improved, always within the boundaries of the fundamental ordering principles, until these are exhausted and have to make room for newer ones which have within themselves the essentials of the older principles.

All these ordering principles lie enclosed in the religious root of nature, and whenever their time comes, they come into effect. Cultural and technical works are signs pointing to the miracle of the *created spirit*. They are no more creations of thought than the miracles of the living nature are creations of life. The spirit manifests itself in these works as a reality created by God.

The fall and re-creation

I spoke of creation as a work of God that was not performed *in* cosmic time, but that brought time with its sequences and dynamic features into being. Included in God's design are two other fundamental possibilities that determine the execution of the design: the fall into sin and the re-creation.

In God's design the fall is a foreseen possibility of man's falling away from the religious root of his being, from the Word and from the law of God. Should man realize this possibility, he would loose his authority over the lower creation and therefore also over his own body. Then sickness, pain, and dissolution would enter into the course of history; the principle of spiritual death would operate in the cosmos.

The paradise story tells us that this fall did indeed take place. The fall is history, the early history of the origin of evil. The fall is the origin of sin, the primordial sin from which all sin streamed into the world and is still streaming in. No single concrete sin can be separated from the fall, which is a changing of the governed into the ungoverned.

Having fallen away from his religious root, the Word of God, man lost sight of the law for his life, and his works were no longer concentrated upon serving his Creator. Man lost command of his own body which became a "natural body," a "body of death," because the life processes were directed no longer by the law of life toward the maintenance of the whole, but by the law of death toward dissolution. Powers once subjected to the spirit in the service of God now withdrew from their proper relationship to the whole. They no longer worked together harmoniously but worked against each other. Here one dominated, there another; where the parts were no longer obedient to the whole, the unity of life was threatened with destruction and death.

It is part of God's plan that his kingdom shall be built, but Satan aims to destroy that kingdom. Satan brings into the world the principle of division, negativity, and unbelief in the power of God's Word and Spirit. Nevertheless, Satan's work has a place in God's design and is made to serve the coming of his kingdom. The unleashing of sin's powers in fact causes God's re-creating grace to be brought into operation, fully revealing his unlimited love and greatness.

Sin is primarily an attitude arising out of a spiritual principle. The created powers and potentialities in the root of nature can never be called sinful, for they function in agreement with their own laws. But where the principle of sin works itself out (and this is the entire cosmos), these powers are no longer directed to a higher purpose by the law of God but are led astray by the law of sin. They serve then no longer as instruments of the Spirit who binds together in an orderly way, but as tools of Satan who breaks

11

things apart and brings devastation into the cosmos.

Because of the fall man has lost sight of the kingdom of God and with it the religious root of the entire cosmos. He now looks for that root in certain created things — matter, life, soul, or spirit — which he absolutizes and wherein he sees the origins of everything else. Fallen man lives in a world of appearances which he believes to be real because he no longer knows the Word of God as the religious root of life, as a law by which he must be directed in all things.

The re-creation restores the original religious root to man's spiritual field of vision by the Word becoming flesh. In Christ the root has become visible again, and God has made man rediscover himself. After the fall we see in Christ man as he was before the fall. That is why Scripture calls Christ not only the image of God, the power and wisdom of God, but also the *second* Adam, the new man, the *new* head of the re-created human race.

In this world two fundamental principles give direction: the spirit of darkness and the spirit of light; death and life; man in sin and man in grace; the lie and the truth; Satan and Christ.

In and through the fall numerous powers have in their innermost meaning placed themselves in the service of darkness. Diseases of the body, of the soul, and of the spirit, wars , epidemics, and catastrophes of nature directed themselves against the kingdom of God. However, through Christ these results of sin are made to serve the coming of his kingdom because he demonstrates his power over creation in healing, in rescuing, and in control over the elements and thereby works faith and repentance in the hearts of men.

The fall brought no change in God's design because the fall was included in the design as a possibility even before the creation began. We must clearly distinguish between what happens in the course of time and the fixed order which lies at the foundation of what happens and indeed makes what happens possible. Thus we have seen that the world order came into being through God's creative work in Christ. This work is itself not subject to the passage of time, but it is brought to completion in the passage of time. Within the original religious root of nature, before the opening up took place in the presence of man's consciousness, all things, events, and acts lie potentially enclosed in the decision of the Creator. In God's single world plan everything has its place and task.

The miracle of providence

By the providence of God we mean his omnipotent and omnipresent wisdom and power whereby he maintains the cosmos after the beginning and the six days of creative activity and leads it to completion. God rested from his creative work on the seventh day, but he had created heaven and earth to bring them to completion. The powers and possibilities that lay enclosed in the decisions of the Creator had to be disclosed in time.

The creating Word through which all things were made in six days was in no way silenced when this work was finished. This Word can be heard to the end of time as it supports all things by its power and wisdom. From ancient times this providential care has been called the *creatio continua,* the continuing creation. However, this term must not be understood to mean that completely new things originated beside those already created. Rather, it must be taken to mean that the Spirit of God continues to cause new things to appear within the framework of the created world order wherein they were potentially enclosed.

Nothing in the cosmos is outside the providence by which God in his design has directed all things to the completion of his kingdom. The creatures with their functions were in every way attuned to each other and worked together in maintaining certain life relationships. A tremendous wealth of designed relationships is maintained from moment to moment in all sorts of creatures in all the realms of nature and also between the various functions of each individual creature.[5] Everything points beyond itself and is directed to a coming completion from which the processes receive their meaning and purpose.

In modern physics the facts speak for a planned coherence of the elemental natural processes. The physicist Planck in his well-known lecture *Religion und Naturwissenschaft,* which speaks of the elementary building blocks of matter, considers it ''an unquestionable conclusion from research in physics that these elementary building blocks of the world structure do not lie side by side in separate groups without a coherence but that they collectively fit together in a certain pattern. In other words, in all of the events of nature a univeral lawfulness reigns which is known to us only to a certain extent.''[6]

Planck refers to the designed order in nature as *miraculous.* The coherence of things is especially clear in the formulation of the principle of the smallest function to which one may attribute the root of an exact natural law. This is so also in modern physics. ''What we must consider, however, as the greatest miracle of all is the fact that the proper formulation of these laws inspires an impression in each unprejudiced individual, viz., the impression that nature is ruled by an ingenious and purposeful will.''[7]

Planck gives an illustration to clarify his point. Whenever the light beam from another star reaches the eye of an observer, the course of this beam will demonstrate a more or less complex series of bendings as a result of the different refractions through the various atmospheric layers (unless the star happens to be precisely perpendicular at the zenith). In the deeper, denser atmospheres the light travels more slowly than in the higher, less dense atmosphere. This refraction is determined by a simple law: of all the paths that lead from the star to the eye of the observer, the light follows just those paths that will bring it to its destination in the shortest possible time (making allowance for the different rates of travel in the different atmospheric layers). It is as if the photons which form the beam behaved like ''rational creatures.'' From all the possible curves, they always choose those which carry them to their destinations most rapidly.

This law, according to Planck, can be applied to all of nature. It is possible to recognize the result of every process in a given physical system with all its characteristic details. The following axiom is observed: out of all the conceivable processes by which in a given time a certain system is transferred from one set of conditions to another set, the real process will be the one for which during this time the extending integral of a certain magnitude possesses the smallest value. ''As a matter of fact, by means of the principle of effect a completely new idea is introduced in the concept of causality: along with the efficient cause, viz., the motive which works out of the present into the future, the final cause is added. The latter alters the future, namely, a determined objective which is strived for. The final cause is made a prerequisite and thus diverts the development of the process which is directed to this objective.''[8]

In astronomy, too, researchers are increasingly recognizing cosmic events. In his book *The Mysterious Universe*, J. Jeans writes:

Today there is a wide measure of agreement which on the physical side of science approaches almost to unanimity, that the stream of knowledge is heading towards a nonmechanical reality; the universe begins to look more like a great thought than like a great machine. Mind no longer appears as an accidental intruder into the realm of matter; we are beginning to suspect that we ought rather to hail it as the creator and governor of the realm of matter — not of course our individual minds, but the mind in which the atoms out of which our individual minds have grown exist as thoughts.[9]

In biology, the recognition of design in biotic processes is gaining ground rapidly. Building on the principles laid down by Driesch, the new experimental embryology, under the pressure of a mounting pile of facts, has abandoned the mechanistic theory of life. It has begun to acknowledge an ordering and harmonizing principle that controls the forming processes during the embryonal development of the creature. Tests have shown that in the young seed the various processes are present in a many-sided mutual interaction. In several publications Vogt points with emphasis to the unity of these processes and to the design with which they are geared to each other. He speaks of a dynamic determination in the young gastrula rather than a mechanistic one. Moreover, in his most recent writing, Spemann says: "The movements are not crudely restricted through the pressure and the pull of single components but they are designed in an orderly manner."[10]

Miraculous also are the relationships between the various kinds of organisms and their living and non-living milieu. I am borrowing the following example from J. von Uexküll's little book *Bedeutungslehre*. When a spider spins a web, every step of the process is directed toward the future even though it is causally determined. The size of the openings is related to the size of the flies to be caught. The resistance of the threads is proportionate to the dynamic power of the flying insect body. The radial threads are spun somewhat stronger than the circular ones so that the fly colliding with the circular threads which give a little is soon surrounded by them and hopelessly imprisoned in their sticky droplets. The radial threads, however, are not sticky and serve the spider as the shortest route to the captured prey, which is then speedily surrounded with more threads and rendered helpless. Furthermore, these webs are made chiefly in spots where many flies can be caught.[11] Perhaps the most remarkable thing of all is that the threads of the webs are spun so finely that the multi-facetted eye of the fly cannot see them. Thus the fly enters the prison without any warning.

Similar inter-relationships occur everywhere in nature. Think, for example, of how various animals and plants are oriented to each other, and how living creatures and the non-living milieu of earth, water, or air are suited to each other. How well every fish, every bird, and every mammal fits into its environment!

Are these remarkable adaptations to be considered the result of natural selection and other mechanistic factors? If so, the principle of chance would be elevated to creative power. The history of life on earth reveals a spontaneous appearance of groups of organisms in designed relationships to each other and to their non-living milieu. Thus during the Cretacious Period the greater part of the reptile phylum died for as yet unknown reasons. Only remnants remain with us today. At the same time a new kind of flora spread quickly over the earth. Thick steppe grasses, fragrant and honey-producing herbs, leafy trees, and fleshy seeds formed the inexhaustable food supply for numerous new groups of animals. Then a very remarkable event took place: at the beginning of the Tertiary Period, many mammals appeared. The formation of extensive ocean depths and the growth of continents by the appearance of gigantic mountain ranges accompanied the lively unfolding, distribution, and differentiation that we see during this time in the flowering plants, the insects, the birds, and the mammals.[12]

Christianity has always confessed that the providence of God extends over all things, including the history of men and nations. Man also is bound to the whole of nature by means of numerous designed relationships. Through faith in the Word and law of God, man was originally able to exercise dominion over nature and to direct the natural processes meaningfully toward a higher goal. Nature was obedient to Adam. It served him, and he opened up its powers and possibilities in the service of fulfilling God's kingdom on earth.

After the fall man had this ability restored to him in principle through Christ. He who believes in Christ with his whole heart, he who in Christ's service places his life with continual trust on God's promises, shall be able to do sensational things in every area of culture. He will be able to do ''signs and miracles'' which are impossible without strong faith and prayer, but only when God calls him for that purpose. The history of Israel and of Christianity is full of examples of such acts. They may be seen in the history of churches, of christian societies, of missionary associations, and of the lives of individual Christians.

The designed relationships between the different kinds of creatures are tokens of God's wise and providential rule. Enclosed in the divine world order, they contain a great wealth of possibilities for the processes of movement, developmental phenomena, and actions and behaviours in all the realms of nature that have to be opened up in cosmic time through individual subjective activity. All these relationships are signs of the miracles of providence from which they cannot be separated and which made their existence possible in the first place.

With the signs and miracles of God's providence in the history of mankind no laws or fixed relationships are circumvented. But under other than the ordinary, well-known conditions, other powers are opened up. This happens when man lives and acts out of faith and prayer. The potentials and powers of nature are thus harnessed in the service of the coming of God's kingdom on earth. The believing Christian, who knows that God's providence reaches out over all things and that nothing is outside his care, will see in signs and miracles the proof of God's promises that nothing shall be impossible to him who believes. Only faith can work signs and miracles and only faith can see them.

The miracle of re-creation
Whenever miracles are discussed from a theological viewpoint, it is almost always the miracles of re-creation which receive

attention. Most of the writing on miracles concerns them, and it is with them that the problem of the relationship between nature and miracles is most likely to come up.

Scripture relates over and over again singular, unexpected events, which seem to clash with the usual order of events or at least depart from laws which experience has discovered. These are always special deliverances, cures, awakenings, and the like by which the kingdom of God is maintained on earth, freed from the results of sin, increased, and led toward perfection. Scripture describes these events as signs and miracles, the miraculous deeds and works of God. They are always seen in relation to the God who performs them: not the gods of the heathen, but only Israel's God can do miracles.

The question may be raised whether the acknowledgment that only God can do miracles means that he then works in a supernatural way interfering with the regular cadence of natural events. He who accepts this concept begins with a belief in an autonomous nature in which he allows God from time to time to operate from the outside as a *deus ex machina*. This way of thinking is absolutely unscriptural.

God re-created the cosmos in Christ as the new religious root of nature. Thereby the original order of the kingdom was once more made apparent to the eyes of fallen man. The powers that after the fall would be used to combat Satan to the end of time and finally to destroy him were already enclosed in this root before the fall. This fundamental and central miracle of re-creation is continuously present and active in Christ and is driven to completion in the passage of time by the Spirit of God. This is the process of sacred history, an impressive unified whole of signs and miracles. The miracle of the new being is revealed in the miraculous signs of the new life and struggle going on in all the realms of nature.

Signs and miracles cannot be separated from each other. Often Scripture mentions them in one breath. Signs and miracles are related as the peripheral and the central, as the outside and the inside of one and the same reality of revelation.

In orthodox protestant circles the concept prevails that God usually works through the laws and powers he put in the creation, but that in the signs and miracles of re-creation he works super-naturally toward the growth of his kingdom. This view occurs in many of the writings of the last forty years. A few examples follow.

Speaking of healing in answer to prayer, S.R. Hermanides accepts an ''intervention of God in the laws of nature or a peculiar guidance of these laws. While the latter is in fact a diversion of the normal operation of the laws of nature, it is an intervention and hence a miracle.'' Before we can establish that such a miracle occurred, '' we must be able to show wherein the supernatural work took place or wherein the particular deviation from the natural working of life forces was effected. Where did an interference in the law take place which cannot be explained in a natural way?'' [13]

H. Woltjer takes the miracles to be ''supernatural events in the sensory world. They contradict all known laws of nature, and there is no hope of bringing them into line with these laws.'' Here we have a ''breaking up of natural laws.'' ''In the miracles of the increase of the loaves and fishes, for example, we detect the supernatural. We feel intuitively that we are dealing here with another order of events. There is just no prospect that we will ever be able to explain this in a scientific way.'' [14]

C.W. Scheffer defines a miracle as ''an unusual event that can be experienced by the senses. It goes beyond the powers of nature, and it has God as its author.'' For him a miracle lies ''beyond the bounds of the powers of nature.'' A certain ''divine arbitrariness'' shows up in it. [15]

F.W. Grosheide speaks of miracles as ''deeds of God in which he acts without regard for the laws and powers which he himself put in nature and without regard for all the statistically possible combinations.... Not only Scripture but also experience teaches that the natural order can be set aside. This is the miracle.'' [16]

J. Bruin is of the opinion that the so-called miracles of nature ''in which the material aspect is deeply involved (e.g., the standing still of the sun, the increase of the loaves of bread, the turning of water into wine) ... are all in conflict with well-known natural laws. They cannot be harmonized with them; therefore, nature is being interfered with.'' A miracle is thus a setting aside of laws. [17]

Writing about the remarkable instances of healing at Möttlingen, P. Jasperse assumes that a kind of psychotherapy was applied there, in which suggestion played a major role. Gottliebin Dittus, healed by Blumhardt, showed typical symptoms of hysteria — symptoms that are psychically grounded and that can also appear under hypnosis. Jasperse maintains that there is no need whatsoever to view this healing process as a direct interference of God. This would also hold for other instances of healing. In a series of articles Jasperse has tried to judge whether or not the phenomena called miracles are really special interventions of God in the natural processes. In other words, do these healings represent God speaking clearly and directly or are they merely processes and powers that God put in nature and that are ''therefore of his making.'' [18]

In an article on healing by faith and prayer, G.A. Lindeboom deals with ''healing from physical illness as a result of prayer alone, without the use of natural means but as a direct act of God." [19] He goes on to say,

The so-called divine healings of which examples are usually mentioned may be termed miraculous. In Pentecostal circles (at Möttlingen, for example), such divine restorations take place as often as they are truly prayed for. This happens among other groups too, especially in England and America. Other Christians, including Catholics, also maintain that such healings take place regularly, although they do not want to be as emphatic about it as the Pentecostal groups.

About Jesus' healing work, Lindeboom continues, the gospel writers record that "all who saw it believed." Today the question asked is this: "Do such healings also occur in our time — healings which everyone, including physicians, must believe and confirm to be of supernatural origin?" The difficulty in the scientific approach to this question, according to Lindeboom, is that medical science as such cannot express itself on the supernatural. It has no way of studying this scientifically. The physician can only say, "Here is a mystery." A great deal has to happen before he is willing to add, "These events go against nature's laws."

Lindeboom adds that not all natural laws are presently known; many secret powers are still hidden away in nature, powers whose working we merely glimpse from time to time. In earlier centuries many events were considered supernatural that to us are so natural that we scarcely give them a thought. Furthermore, as the knowledge of natural laws increases, many phenomena will lose their miraculous character.

In his argument Lindeboom next points to the influence of the psyche on the processes of life, including healing. Again and again the psyche suddenly comes forward with the ability to overcome illness. When we consider the work of the spirit, in addition to the unconscious working of the psyche, the relationships become very complex. The spirit often works not only pathogenically but also therapeutically with great power. Both functional and purely organic abnormalities can submit to the power of the spirit. Think of the influence of suggestion and hypnosis. Lindeboom notes:

It is always true that the anticipated recovery is of great importance in the actual recovery of a suffering person. Now and again the importance of that faith in recovery is shown in a miraculous way. Such a faith is usually religiously oriented, but it does not have to have anything in common with christian faith. That healing can follow anyway is substantiated by the votive sculptures saved from ancient Greece, and by reports of recoveries from far away India and from western lands as well.

It may be a faith healer, a relic, or the bone of a saint to which the miraculous recoveries are ascribed, but it is always *through faith* that tumors disappear and great sores heal.

19

It serves the interest of no one, not even Christians, says Lindeboom, to call natural recoveries miraculous. It is not a question of God's ability to do miracles but of his willingness. If we consider faith healings at Möttlingen critically, it will be hard to find a physician who upon reading about them says, "Here every natural explanation falls short." For us these events are no reason to start talking about the direct intervention of God. Lindeboom agrees to a great extent with Jasperse's critical analysis of these recoveries.

However, in Lourdes "miraculous things" actually happen. Here faith healing has the characteristics of divine healing. The events happen suddenly. Recoveries from sores, festering wounds, tuberculosis, and cancer take place at once. But Lindeboom says there remains something to be desired in the matter of medical control. One cannot just accept these recoveries as supernatural. The person who goes to Lourdes moves in a cloud of faith and is greatly excited by hope. Still, some cases of miraculous recoveries remain. If they are not miracles, they are extremely curious. Lindeboom says that he cannot see why Protestants will not eventually recognize the miraculous recoveries at Lourdes as results of prayer.

From the preceding summaries it is clear that among believing Protestants the miraculous character of the healing works of Jesus and his disciples recounted in Scripture is seen as supernatural intervention. Moreover, along with the recognition that these biblical cures are "real" miracles goes considerable doubt about the supernatural nature of the cures at Lourdes, Möttlingen, and so on. They stress that the unconscious working of the psyche can greatly influence the corporal processes. Furthermore, Lindeboom thinks that "the effects of post-hypnotic suggestion are far greater than we think at present." Scheffer maintains that little is known about the limits of psychic influence on the somatic processes. With the exception of raising the dead, he feels that "the boundaries where natural processes stop are impossible to establish." When he talks about the cures at Möttlingen, Jasperse discusses the powers God put in nature. Scheffer says there is as yet no proof that miracles happened at Lourdes.

Prompted by the articles of these physicians, I wish to say first of all that scientific proof for the miraculous character of an event can never be given. Lindeboom acknowledges this. When one starts by identifying miracle with the supernatural, one can never expect to discover anything by research. If it is done critically, scientific research admits only the causes and the possibilities of the created order. The created spirit of man belongs here also. The investigator can never claim that a supernatural event occurred mainly because it is unusual. Since authors I cited earlier also acknowledge this, I find Scheffer's conclusion arbitrary when he says that rising from the dead is beyond the realm of natural possibility. Should someone be raised from the dead some day — and I do not consider this impossible — then the researcher has no right to look for a supernatural explanation. He ceases to be a scientist when he does so and becomes a metaphysician. And metaphysics is the greatest enemy of scientific research, indeed, of all truth and of all true religion.

When we explain the miraculous by the supernatural, the miraculous is in fact denied. I fear that a number of contemporary Christians, with their concept of miracles as supernatural and with their knowledge of present-day medicine and psychology, would doubt the miraculous character of the cures told about in Scripture if these occurred in Europe today. Supernatural events neither occurred in Palestine then, nor do they occur in Europe today.

Scientifically enlightened Protestants of our time scarcely see "real" miracles in nature anymore. They have pushed them back far into the past into Bible times where they are safe from scientific criticism as if they were in a bomb shelter. They maintain that the miracles of the Bible were caused by divine intervention and cannot be reduced to natural powers. Any other explanation is considered out of the question.

We are dealing here with the remnants of the old supernaturalism present in eighteenth-century orthodox protestant circles. This supernaturalism had been developed in opposition to Deism, which had been built on the foundation of a rationally conceived nature cut loose from its religious root, the Word and Spirit of God. [20] At that time, under the influence of the rapidly rising natural science, the so-called miracles of nature were limited to a number of divine deeds in the past. Men began with the idea that God caused ordinary natural events through powers he has put in nature. Thus God worked by means of natural laws as a rule, but in miracles he intervened super-naturally by setting aside certain laws. Protestant believers who were scientifically oriented maintained that God had established a fixed order for all natural events and that nothing could depart from this order. And such Protestants think this way to this very day. Since the eighteenth century, however, they have discovered the working of the unconscious psyche and the conscious spirit, which manifest themselves in numerous natural events that were once either unknown or scarcely known, and they consider these explainable as powers God put in nature. In this area they are very skeptical of miracles.

This position, taken by many christian physicians and

scientists, is also a reaction against the super-natural view of miracles in Roman Catholic circles. Catholicism has always been inclined to conceive of God as acting supernaturally in nature, when events occur that are beyond comprehension by the average man and explanation by the scientific people of the time. Protestants see the Roman Catholic views partly as superstition and partly as an explanation that unnecessarily calls in unknown powers beyond man's control. Many phenomena which were considered supernatural yesterday can be scientifically explained today. Yet miracles, like a number of the cures at Lourdes, continue to happen. Catholicism calls them supernatural, but protestant believers deny this explanation, and rightly so. The supernatural was, is and always will be an *asylum ignorantiae,* into which one can push anything and everything and which cannot be explained.

When a believing Protestant thinks he has to uphold a supernatural explanation of the miracles in the Bible, he arbitrarily separates miraculous phenomena of the past from those of the present. Supernaturalism has been pushed aside more and more by rapidly developing scientific research. The bomb shelter for supernaturalism is under attack and will certainly suffer some direct hits in the future. In many instances Jesus' miraculous cures have remarkably similar parallels today. [21] In the gospels we often read of cures from diseases that in essence have nervous or psychic causes and involve deviations and impediments in the functioning of the nervous system. We read about the restoration of the mentally ill, the lame, and those suffering from leprosy or prolonged flow of blood. Deafness, blindness, and muteness are also often of psychic origin; current psychotherapy records many instances of cures from such illnesses.

However, Scripture also tells us of many cures which at present do not have parallels. Because supernaturalism will certainly fall back on these to defend its position, two things must be kept in mind. In the first place, it has never been proven that supernatural power is needed to effect miracles such as raising the dead. Second, it is very well possible that cures of this sort — even raising the dead — may take place in our day or in the near future.

Furthermore, even the nature miracles of Jesus and his disciples, in which extraordinary control of the elements is shown, have their parallels in our time. I am thinking of the numerous facts of parapsychology and the practices of Indian yogis in particular. Through long practice these people are capable of developing various supernormal abilities that are not pathological in nature. Examples of these skills are clairvoyance in time and space, levitation, fire swallowing, and ability to become invisible. Some are able to walk on water or through solid structures and walls. They can change their body weight arbitrarily or take on more than one body. They can appear to be dead and can be buried only to awake later from these cataleptic states and arise from the grave. That at least some of these abilities also exist among westerners has been established under strict scientific controls. [22] Parapsychology, while it acknowledges the miraculous nature of these phenomena, would not even consider explaining them as supernatural.

I am convinced that it is not at all necessary to posit supernatural intervention as an explanation for the miracles that Scripture relates. Anyone who uses supernaturalism as an explanation cuts himself off from gaining insight into the real nature of these events. When Jesus commands the elements he does so by his natural authority over them. They are placed in the service of God's kingdom and are obedient to its directing powers. How all this happened remains hidden from us as yet. When reading these accounts, we must remember that the biblical authors wrote down their naive experiences. They simply reported what happened without pretending to give an explanation or to expose the causes. This is a task reserved for science.

Before we can gain a clear insight into the relationship between re-creation and nature, we must make a radical departure from the deistic view of nature. "Nature" is nothing by itself. From moment to moment it is upheld by the power and wisdom of God through his Word and Spirit and cannot be separated from them. Calvin saw that nature is an order directed by God within which the lower aspects of his work occur. In Scripture nature is often referred to in this way.

But God did not make this order autonomous to bring about the natural course of events. Rather, this order is the fixed law to which God himself in his Covenant bound himself in the execution of his plan. This must not be understood to mean that God is subject to the created order but that he now personally works out the created fulness of the order, in order to complete in Christ what he began to create and re-create in Christ. It is God himself who does everything in nature. God himself directs all things to their destined ends in the service of his coming kingdom. All ordered material, organic, psychic, or spiritual phenomena, whether or not they are called miraculous, are enclosed in the religious root of nature by the Word and Spirit and are pushed forth from this root in the course of time.

From a scriptural point of view, it is not justifiable to distinguish between direct works of God when considering the signs and wonders, and indirect works when considering the so-called ordinary phenomena of nature. G.J. Sizoo is entirely right when he says that it is also in the ordinary daily run of events that the Word of God is evident. Even Scripture calls what we experience as normal natural phenomena the direct deeds of God. [23]

The ''powers of nature'' cannot be separated from God and thought of as working on their own. They must continually be seen as dependent on him from whom they come. They are a manifold expression of one and the same power of God that reveals itself in all things. God's deeds are continuously direct. He performs numerous miraculous deeds — signs and wonders. He makes the storm and the rain and the snow; he brings thunder and lightning; he fills the sky with clouds; he causes earthquakes and volcanic eruptions; he causes the grass in the meadows to sprout, the seed to germinate, and the bud to flower; he pushes the ants to gather food and makes lions roar; he makes man to will and to work in keeping with his divine plan. And whenever it fits this divine plan, God also performs signs and wonders of re-creation in great number to destroy the works of Satan.

I can therefore agree entirely with L. van der Horst that the Bible believer

…even when he grants that the occult appearances can possibly be explained by unknown natural laws or by spiritual powers in man, still sees God's power in these events. God's miracles are continually revealed to us in nature…. If we continue to feel our dependence, if there is a willingness to wait for the miracles, then we will see them everywhere about us in the usual run of natural events…. We see God's power plainly in world occurrences. With every flower that opens, with every baby born, with every cure of the mentally sick a miracle occurs.[24]

The task of science is to show the fixed structural laws and designed relationships within which things appear in time. Science makes abstractions from the whole and from the root and studies particular aspects and areas. The phenomena that science studies are always bound to certain conditions, and the rules and laws which it discovers and formulates hold only under those conditions. Thus, for example, the laws of macro-physical phenomena are valid only when one deals with massive events; only under this condition can they become manifest. Granted this condition, they allow no exceptions and are never suspended. For the believing Christian this is a proof of God's faithfulness to his creation. Under other conditions we find other laws. For example, there are the laws for atomic processes, for living processes, and for different aspects of man's spirit as well.

We must break radically not only with the deistic conception of nature but also with the supernaturalistic conception of miracles. The miracle of re-creation is worked by God in Christ Jesus. No signs and wonders can be divorced from this central miracle. The words and works of Christ are so many signs and wonders which reveal the central re-creation miracle of the new order. In this order power over creation has been restored to man. Luther rightly says that the life of Jesus is a continuous miracle, a continuous revelation of the law of the kingdom that directs all his words and acts.

All the signs and wonders that Jesus performs are perfectly natural for him. He does them in the power of his divine nature as Creator, Providential Guide, and Re-creator of the cosmos. However, his human nature cannot be separated from his divine nature. It is a fulness of created powers and abilities that manifest themselves as signs and wonders through the work of the Spirit. Christ's nature — man and God in one — is the root from which all his miraculous deeds come.

The signs and wonders of Christ did not meddle with natural events nor set laws aside. What happened, and still happens, is that the lower natural processes, preserving their peculiar laws, again obey the guidance of a higher order, the law of service to God's kingdom. Whenever the original law of Christ is restored, we see miraculous potentialities emerge as the elements are withdrawn from the destructive power and influence of sin and are led anew in their proper courses. Thus, as in paradise, they no longer threaten man.

It is not only Jesus who could perform miracles while he was on earth; all those bound to him by true faith can perform them too. Christ has chosen his own since the time of Paradise to do great things in his name, the signs and wonders that will break the power of Satan. In Scripture we find many illustrations of this from Genesis to Revelation. In reality it is always Christ who by his Word and Spirit performs these signs and wonders: conversions, cures, rescues, raising the dead, control of the elements, and so on. In the signs and wonders certain powers and abilities, enclosed in the religious root of nature, are brought into operation *under specific conditions.* The resulting natural and spiritual phenomenon would not have occurred without those conditions being met.

Through the signs and wonders the disintegrating power of sin is broken and its results overcome. What occurs is not a supernatural interference in the positive consequence of a natural process, but a fully natural interference in the negative consequence of a sinful process. The elementary natural processes become directed toward their destiny in obedience to the law of service to God, just as the acts of man's spirit are so directed. Nothing happens against nature but only against sin and its results. G. Brillenburg Wurth rightly says that the miracles of

Jesus are neither supernatural nor against nature. "They do not go against nature but against the sinful state of nature which has become so by demonic powers, sickness, and such. Going against the sinful state of nature, these miracles actually restore the original state of nature." [25]

Faith and prayer as conditions

As the conditions under which signs and wonders of re-creation are possible, I mentioned great faith and earnest prayer, whether conscious or unconscious. That faith is necessary to accomplish miracles Scripture makes clear. In faith and prayer man stands entirely open to the re-creating work of God's Spirit which can unlock in him great abilities for fighting sin and mastering nature. The conversion of a sinner is a great and central miracle which will manifest itself in his actions. Increasingly his life will become a sign of the spiritual reality of God's kingdom. The more fallen man becomes an instrument of Christ, the greater will be the signs he may perform. Consider, for example, Moses, Elijah, Paul, and many others. At present, indeed at all times, the signs and wonders of re-creation are evident. We see them in the life and work of innumerable believers in the various church denominations. We see them at Möttlingen and Lourdes and wherever faith and prayer make possible the impossible.

In this connection, J.L. de Heer wrote that every sickness is really a symptom of the sin-sickness of the soul and can be radically cured only by rebirth and conversion. When Jesus cured sin-sickness, the signs and wonders followed whenever these fitted in with his re-creation plan. "Today similar signs and wonders also follow the whole gamut of illnesses when the physician applies not only symptomatic but also etiological sin-sickness therapy. Through Christ, the Great Physician, the doctor becomes more useful in Christ's plan for the patient." [26]

E. Liek gives us the following striking example of signs and wonders through faith. [27] One of Liek's colleagues was the head of a clinic at Banjaluka in North Bosnia for thirteen years. He witnessed the events recounted here and told them to Liek. While in Bosnia Liek's colleague had many problems to solve. Austria-Hungary had taken over the province straight from the Turks. Because there were few doctors in the land, people looked after themselves and depended on the experience of the centuries. The doctor tells the following:

"I often admired the farmers and was amazed how they courageously helped themselves. Often I was ashamed when I saw that their expectations rose far too high whenever our doctors visited them. The number of doctors remained too small, so that in general the masses were left to themselves and the chronically sick were not treated. Pain undermined the autonomic nervous system of robust fellows, and thus there developed a host of neurotics who suffered from neurasthenic disorders, especially hysteria, and who wanted to be helped. The treatment of the masses in hospitals was such that one had to be grateful to stay alive. Truly one could seldom, if ever, help the people. Because of this situation an interesting task fell to me on a certain day. I want to tell you about it because of its relationships to 'quackery' and 'magic.'

"About thirty-five miles south of Banjaluka stood a lone and tiny, old church dedicated to St. John and near it a parsonage. The little church seemed to be empty and forgotten all year round. Only on St. John's Day, June 24, was it lively thereabouts.

Thousands of pilgrims streamed in at this time, for, as in the time of Ekkehard, the Franciscan fathers cast out devils on this day."

The doctor continues that the governor of the Banjaluka District had asked him to come and see this expulsion of devils and to judge whether or not this practice ought to be banned because it no longer fitted in the times. On June 23 he went to the place. "Franciscans sat on the grave mounds bent over toward the farmers and their wives who knelt before them and toward them. 'What does this mean?' I asked. The answer was, 'This evening and all through the night all who want devils cast out in the morning make confession.'

"This scene made a deep impression on me. We rode on to the place where we would spend the night and returned the next morning. The letter of introduction from the bishop made it possible for me to get through the crowd, although with difficulty. At last I could take my place behind the priest. There was a movement in the crowd. One heard screams from a distance. Someone brought a woman with a distorted face before the priest. Emphatically he pronounced the centuries-old formula of exorcism; as in Ekkehard's time, he cried, 'Exi!, Exi!' and repeatedly thrust the cross in the direction of the woman. She became visibly calmer. The priest paused a moment and, turning in my direction, said, 'A serious case. I have driven out some devils but one or two still remain in her!' He continued his incantation, and the woman stopped screaming and finally began to talk again. While the exorcism was going on, every cry of the priest was taken up by the believing mass like an echo of a hundred tense and hopeful voices. The believing, cooperating people in the church pushed forward in a wave in the direction of the priest. The incense and mystical semi-darkness added their effect. Cured at last, the woman walked joyfully out of the church. Many another burdened soul also felt a weight lifted from his heart because he too had seen and experienced how she and others had been aided and relieved.

"Thus it went on. I had seen and experienced enough and could no longer bear the heat, so I left the church. That noon I had been invited to eat at the parish priest's house. There I found many Franciscan priests eating a meal and talking over the morning's events amongst themselves. I listened attentively and looked closely, but I never heard a cynical word or saw a mocking smile. Indeed, a cultured and robust young priest said to the slighter father who had performed the excorcisms that morning, 'You have not been able to drive out all the devils today. Last year I did, but then my faith is stronger than yours.'"

When the doctor returned home he advised the governor to do nothing against these exorcisms. "After all at the time we had not a single institution for neurological or psychiatric illnesses." The story he told to Liek ends: "I enthusiastically respond to your remarks about a true physician's use of magic, in connection with these events. To phrase it along the lines of the gospel, 'Truly I say to you, the poor priest in that tiny forsaken church was a good physician on St. John's Day. He was a thousand times better than the army of medical personnel who would have sent the poor screaming woman home uncured and uncomforted and who, moreover, would have contemptuously labelled her 'hysterical.'

"Today these pilgrimages and exorcisms still go on every St. John's Day. The spell still accomplishes cures and relief."

Only in faith can man perform signs and wonders, but it is just as true that only faith can see them. The scientific worker can deal only in concepts such as hysteria, suggestion, hypnosis and hallucination. He is obliged to take the phenomena and show that they have natural causes; he may never resort to explaining them by supernatural factors. But in this way he will never be able to find traces of a miraculous cure accomplished through faith or of a miraculous deliverance in answer to prayer. However, when he contends that there are no signs and wonders because he is unable to find them, he is guilty of absolutizing abstract laws, powers, and abilities. He cannot explain scientifically the *possibility* of the existence and function of either non-living or living things but simply has to start with the facts of their existence and function as he goes about his research. In the same way he can never give an explanation of the possibility of restoration from sickness and deliverance from danger as a result of faith and prayer. He does an injustice to reality by forcing it into a preconceived scheme of abstract concepts when he refuses to begin by accepting the facts just mentioned as complete experiential reality. If he wants a complete understanding of all these facts, he will have to start with the miracles of creation, providence, and re-creation. He will have to begin with believing.

Re-creation is universal

Christians are not the only people who experience remarkable cures and deliverances or are able to do miraculous things because of their strong faith. These experiences have occurred also among ''heathens'' in all ages. Nevertheless, all these cures and deliverances have in common the great faith of the people involved and their unshakable conviction that they will certainly be helped if they follow the instructions given by a person they trust. They lay themselves open to powers of restoration and deliverance, whether these come from people or from supposed supernatural powers. According to Liek, the witch doctor distributes and dispenses power; therein lies the secret of his success. The power that goes out from him is the faith and trust he inspires. Trust is the strongest bond between doctor and patient. The witch doctor believes in his own abilities and the patient believes in him. To him who believes, says Jesus, nothing is impossible.

In all these more or less miraculous cures the miracle of re-creation is revealed. They are the signs through which this central miracle becomes visible. God worked this central miracle in the religious root of creation and now works it out in the course of time. To put it more forcefully, *all* healing powers of all times and of all peoples proceed from this basis. That does not mean that everyone who is cured sees God's hand in operation. It may be that he believes in the power of Aesculapius, a relic, a witch doctor, a priest, or a layman gifted with healing powers. But he *believes*. He believes in the miracle and in the possibility of the restoration of his disturbed functions.

We can even go a step further. Wherever restoration of order is experienced in nature, the miracle of the re-creating Word is revealed. We see the Word working also in the animal world where suffering from wounds, sickness, and degeneration has appeared because of sin. The sick animal sighs unconsciously and strives for relief and the restoration of its disturbed functions. This drive often results in very remarkable phenomena of regeneration, in which the injured body uses existing materials for new growth patterned as much as possible on the original. The regenerating impulses are directed toward the whole, toward the maintenance of the life relationships. They point to the authority that a designed spiritual order has over the elementary physical and chemical powers.

This principle is illustrated by the well-known experiments which Driesch performed on various animals at different stages of their development. In the ascidias Clavellina he separated the branchial basket from the sac which contains it; he discovered that each part could produce the other from out of the wound. But the branchial basket can also lose its organized form until it looks like a white cone and is only two cell layers thick with some connective tissue between them. This cone is then reorganized again and forms a very small but complete Clavellina. Furthermore, if a branchial basket is isolated and then cut into two parts, each of these parts is capable of developing into a small, complete Clavellina. Many similar experiments have been done by several different researchers.

In the plant world we also find many examples of regeneration. A complete plant can develop from each epidermal cell located along the vein of an isolated begonia leaf. In certain liverworts or algae almost every cell of the mature plant can develop into a complete plant.

Even in the mineral world we see the work of the re-creating Word. If we take the top off an alum crystal and return it to the solution, it regenerates the top before it continues to grow. If we polish the alum crystal until it is cone-shaped, it readily grows back into a small octagon.

Now all these things may perhaps be explained on the basis of physiological or of physical and chemical laws. However, the *fact* that the order is restored must be recognized before one begins to expose by causal analysis the lawfully operating powers.

The law of sin leads to meaninglessness

The law of dissolution and the law of re-creation can be understood only *spiritually*. There are many examples of developmental processes which led to pathological phenomena and meaninglessness. Certain parts and partial processes made themselves autonomous and did not submit themselves to the designed order of the whole. Thus, for example, after an amputation spontaneous super-regeneration sometimes occurs with superfluous arms or legs, heads or tails. Another example is the *differentiation* of an ovarian growth into sebaceous glands, hair, skin, spinal marrow, or some layers of brain tissue.

Sometimes certain processes go into abnormal developmental pathways during the embryonal period. The result is every kind and degree of abnormality in body structure. To illustrate this, let me give the following example. An anatomical investigation of a rare and serious case of spina bifida with anterior and posterior congenital fissure led me to study forty similar cases from the medical literature of the last one hundred years. From these cases one can trace step by step the working out of the law of dissolution.

In the least serious cases of spina bifida, a small, barely visible vertebral fissure occurs through an area of from one to five vertebrae. The defective area is closed by a membrane, and the central nervous system is intact. Functionally the worst that happens is a disturbance of some autonomic processes. The next most serious stage includes cases with cysts or tumors in the fissure. Although the nervous system is usually intact, the chances that the fetus will live decrease.

The third stage involves cases with an open spinal canal, either limited to part of the vertebral column or continuing through the length of the column. This is rhachischisis posterior, in which the vertebral marrow is more or less degenerate and the skull and brain usually show similar defects. The fetus cannot live. Rhachischisis posterior may be accompanied by rhachischisis anterior, in which the body of the vertebrae is also split. The forty cases I mentioned belong to this group. There are defects in nearly all the internal organs; the greater the fissure, the worse the disorder. The abdominal organs bulge up into the thoracic cavity because the diaphragm is not closed. In the most serious cases these abdominal organs even push out through the fissure in the cervical vertebrae. The thoracic organs thereby come under pressure and are displaced. If the fissure is in the lumbar region, the organs push out there. Sometimes internal parts are missing and malformed limbs often occur.

One can explain these phenomena genetically as disturbances in the earliest stages of embryonal development and relate these in turn to hereditary factor. But the senselessness of all these destructive cases is not clarified in this manner. Science remains silent about this, and rightly so, for science does not have the means to speak out about this aspect of these events. In earlier centuries people thought the mother of such a fetus was bewitched or had slept with the devil. Now we laugh about this, for who now believes such medieval explanations?

What I have just related, however, can also be considered *spiritually*. In these occurrences we see the negative working of the law of sin which pulls the parts away from the order of the whole and leads to ever greater degrees of disorganization. From the outset the spirit of darkness strives to turn the miracle of creation into a disorderly rubbish heap.

False miracles

We have been talking about the signs and wonders of creation, providence, and re-creation. The Scriptures also speak of the miracles of the anti-Christ and of those who put themselves in the service of the realm of darkness. This is the realm of magic and enchantment and false miracle in which a man consciously makes himself a tool of Satan. These signs oppose God's kingdom or at least impede its coming. Man opens himself to dark, demonic influences that occupy his body and rule it temporarily, often with disastrous results to his organic and psychic health.

We must distinguish between the super-normal abilities some people have and the use they make of these abilities. Abilities such as telekinesis (moving objects from a distance), psychometry (describing events in the past from an object), telepathy, clairvoyance into the past and future, suggestion, hypnosis, hallucinations, magnetism, exorcism of spirits, levitation, fire walking, and so on are natural and not necessarily pathological. They can be put to the service of relieving man's suffering or discovering the earth's treasures (minerals, water). The labour of those who do this serves the coming of the kingdom of God on earth. It is my conviction that Jesus possessed these super-normal abilities when he as a real man became like us in all things, sin excepted. He used these abilities whenever it served the coming of the kingdom.

Why is it that we are usually so reluctant to grant even the possibility that these super-normal abilities played a role in the biblical miracles? We hesitate because these abilities are so often and easily given over to the service of sin. We see this in a number of media such as spiritual seances and in the practices of yogis, fakirs, and other magicians. The super-normal abilities are isolated and made autonomous. They are sold in shows or used to satisfy an unjustifiable curiosity about man's life after death. The abilities are not directed to a higher purpose through a positive spiritual principle but are negatively directed through dark powers. In time this leads to organic, psychic, and ethical dislocation. They do not serve to build up but to tear down God's creative work. The Scripture designates such signs as earthly, natural, devilish, or "false wonders."

Therefore we must distinguish between these signs and the abilities which became apparent in the signs. What is true of all natural abilities is true here: nothing is unclean of itself and for believers all things work together for good.

Miracles and present-day natural science

In the course of this discussion I have pointed out several times that today scientists in physics, biology, medicine, and psychology are speaking of miracles once again. The period of positivism in science and of modernism in worship is receding into the past. Super-normal abilities are being studied scientifically. More and more philosophers acknowledge that they cannot function without a hypothesis of direction-giving factors. They are introducing such concepts as design and purpose, integrality and totality, entelechy and finality, and creative potencies. They speak of a will to live, a will to power, or a will to existence that works behind all things in nature. Vitalism and holism are becoming more popular in various forms.

Contemporary natural science no longer pretends to give a world explanation. Since Heisenberg, it has given up the illusion that it could in theory explain nature causally. This came about because scientists were forced to relinquish the concept of the indissoluble relationship between two successive states of the atom. They abandoned the dogma of the closed state of material nature and allowed the possibility that atomic processes might be led by a higher order.

Consequently, natural science has made room for the peculiarities of living phenomena. To many people this means bringing in the concept of miracle. The essence of the miracle, says P.A. Dietz, is that it goes beyond the causal, beyond the logically understood. Thus it is not an ''explainable'' concept. Dietz maintains that modern natural science has accepted the miraculous character of the world. The living world liberates itself in part from the set of conditions of the material world. ''Life is the miracle of matter.'' Furthermore, the spiritual world frees itself in part from the conditions of the living world — ''the spirit is the miracle of life.'' Dietz continues by saying that this is in nowise an ''absolute'' miracle as theology defines it. For him the miracle is relative. It is great or small according to the degree it has achieved freedom from restrictive conditions. The new concept of miracles is related to the older theological one in the same way as the physical concept of probability is related to one of rigid determination.

Dietz maintains that this wonderful world is built of law and miracle:

The law is the fixed frame which allows it to be measured more or less. It is that upon which one can depend. It is the security that makes the world livable and also the binding fate which admits of a tragic side. Miracle, however, gives the world purpose and meaning. While it gives meaning it also brings the antithesis to the world as a physical entity. The miracle breaks through the closed system of physical laws only to lead to a new system of rigid forms. Out of the opposition of miracle and law the world becomes a living world. A world of mere law would be meaningless; a world of only miracle unthinkable. A neccessary condition for the existence of the world is its law, its being tied down in some way. The condition needed for it to be a living world is the breaking of this law. [28]

On the one hand, Dietz's concept of natural law and miracle represents an advance over the tenets of supernaturalism. He recognizes the openness of the world from lower to higher modes and emphasizes that certain laws are valid only under certain conditions and that on a higher level other laws operate, which are built on those of the lower levels. Moreover, Dietz does not deny the miraculous character of the so-called ordinary phenomena of nature, and he considers the miraculous phenomena of para-psychology to be bound to certain natural conditions. In his concept there remains a place for spontaneity and freedom in the world and for meaningful direction that increases from the lower to the higher levels.

On the other hand, something is lost with Dietz's concept. Miracle has lost the religious meaning that it still possesses in supernaturalism. This meaning is completely relativized: phenomena are miracles only in comparison to phenomena of a lower level whose laws are easier for man's mind to grasp. Thus Dietz talks of the miracle as breaking a certain law. He places the miracle in opposition to the law, as a relative freedom opposed to relative confinement, as relative spontaneity opposed to relative determination.

And herein lies my objection to Dietz's concept of the miracle. He has detached the miracle from the absolute miracles of creation, providence, and re-creation. Within these miracles lie all the signs of the miraculous which appear in the course of time in various parts of the cosmos. Thus life phenomena have indeed a miraculous character. But their miraculous character does not lie in the breaking away from the laws of matter. It lies in their designed order, whereby the material processes are meaningfully directed in the service of the life processes that are in turn directed by a higher law, and finally by the law of the coming kingdom of Christ. No single lower law can be loosened from this highest law.

A miracle is not a breaking away from the lower law. It is a higher law which upholds the lower and directs it beyond itself to a higher purpose.

The miracles of creation, providence, and re-creation are absolute. In the signs and wonders, however, there is a greater and a lesser. The miracle of creation reveals itself more in the structure of plants than in the structure of material nature and still more in the structure of the animal world. It is even greater in the structure of the human race in body, soul, and spirit. But it is in the structure of the body of Christ, of the church, and of the kingdom of God that the miracle of creation is revealed most resplendently.

In the same way, the miracle of providence is revealed more in the designed relationship of organic and psychic living phenomena with the world of matter, where physical-chemical processes serve the development of life, than in the relationship of matter and space. It is even greater in the orderly inter-relatedness of the human spirit with all of lower nature, whereby man's spirit can guide and direct natural events according to higher laws. Greatest of all the signs and wonders of providence is the designed inter-relationship of the Word of God with all that is created. In this relationship the Word directs the temporal events in accordance with the law of the kingdom.

Finally, we see the miracle of re-creation manifest itself to a larger degree in the regeneration in the plant and animal worlds than in the configuration of crystals. An even greater sign of re-creation is the cure and restoration of human bodies. But the miracle of re-creation reveals itself most mightily in man's conversion, the radical release from and cure of the sin-sickness of the soul.

A christian science will come into being only when it begins by radically banishing all philosophical ideas which are not scriptural. A christian science will come into being when it makes Revelation its starting-point. It will take concepts such as miracle, totality, design, purposefulness, potentiality, freedom of the will, and the like and test them against its own fundamental motive [*grondmotief*] of creation, fall, and re-creation. These concepts, which at present are found in the literature more and more, may possibly be accepted but never without testing them. In most cases these concepts have been detached from the miracle of creation, providence, and re-creation and therefore also from the root of all things, from the central absolute miracle of Revelation: Jesus Christ, for whom, through whom, and to whom are all things.

Notes

1. "Wortel der natuur" translated as the "religious root of nature" or the "radical base of nature." The emphasis is on the integral religious character of nature as opposed to the dualism of the natural/supernatural view of nature. (Tr. note)

2. Hugh Miller, **The Footprints of the Creator**, the third London edition (Boston, 1851), pp. 301-302. The original quotation is from a translation by D. Lubach under the title **Het Scheppingswonder**, published in 1863.

3. See H. Conrad-Martius, **Ursprung and Aufbau des lebendigen Kosmos**, 1938.

4. Ibid., pp. 325-339.

5. See p. 83 Vol. III of Herman Dooyeweerd's **A New Critique of Theoretical Thought**. In discussing the three kingdoms of pre-logical qualification, he mentions the plants and their bio-milieu, animals and their symbiotic relationships.

6. M. Planck, **Religion and Naturwissenschaft**, 1938, p. 21.

7. Ibid., p. 24.

8. Ibid., p. 26.

9. J. Jeans, **The Mysterious Universe** (Cambridge, 1937), p. 137.

10. H. Spemann, **Experimentelle Beiträge zu einer Theorie der Entwicklung**, 1936. Diemer stresses particularly the importance of the last chapter.

11. J. von Uexküll, "Bedeutungslehre," **Bios** 10 (1940), pp. 19-20.

12. See Conrad-Martius, **Ursprung und Aufbau**, p. 138.

13. S.R. Hermanides, "Gebedsgenezing uit philosophisch standpunt beschouwd," **Orgaan Chr. Vereen. Nat. Geneesk.** 1904, pp.68ff.

14. H. Woltjer, "Het Wonder," **Orgaan**, 1921, pp. 64-70.

15. C.W. Scheffer, "Het Wonder," **Orgaan**, 1921, pp. 73-74.

16. F.W. Grosheide, "Het Wonder," **Orgaan**, 1923, pp. 6-14.

17. J.Bruin, **Het christelijk geloof en de beoefening der natuurwetenschap**, 1932, pp. 118-135.

18. P. Jasperse, "Geloofsgenezingen in Möttlingen?" **Reformatie** (Oct./Nov. 1935).

19. G.A. Lindeboom, **Geloof en gebedsgenezing** (Ref. Veren. v. Geest. Volksgezondheid, 1937), pp. 27-47.

20. Diemer deals with the problem of the relationship between nature and miracle in a series of outlines in **Philosophia Reformata** beginning in the third quarter of 1943.